DELTA TIME

DELTA TIME

MISSISSIPPI PHOTOGRAPHS BY KEN LIGHT

WITH A FOREWORD BY ROBERT MOSES

SMITHSONIAN INSTITUTION PRESS · WASHINGTON AND LONDON

Foreword © 1995 by Robert Moses
"Ella's Song," composed by Bernice Johnson Reagon,
Songtalk Publishing Co., used by permission.

Library of Congress Cataloging-in-Publication Data

Ken Light.
Delta time : Mississippi photographs / by Ken Light :
with a foreword by Robert Moses.
p.   cm.
ISBN 1-56098-470-8 (cloth). — ISBN 1-56098-469-4 (paper).
1. Delta (Miss. : Region)—Social life and customs—Pictorial works.
I. Title.
F347.M6L54   1994
976.2'1-dc20   9425891

British Library Cataloging-in-Publication data available

Manufactured in the United States of America
00 99 98 97 96 95   5 4 3 2 1

∞ The paper used in this publication meets the minimum requirements
of the American National Standard for Permanence of Paper
for Printed Library Materials Z39.48-1984.

Cover illustration: Mr. Bucklesy. Shelby, Mississippi, 1990.
Frontispiece: Plantation shack in cotton field. Mississippi Delta, 1990.

CONTENTS

VII
ACKNOWLEDGMENTS

XI
FOREWORD BY BOB MOSES

1
PHOTOGRAPHS

121
AFTERWORD BY KEN LIGHT

126
TECHNICAL INFORMATION

THIS BOOK IS DEDICATED TO THOSE WHO FOUGHT FOR JUSTICE
AND TO THOSE WHO CONTINUE...

ACKNOWLEDGMENTS

This book would not have been possible without the support of friends and family. I want to especially thank my wife and partner, Melanie. Her continuing encouragement and support helped me get through the last part of this project. Her advice, eye, and love were always there whenever they were needed.

Special thanks go to my colleagues at the Minority Journalism Program at the Institute of Journalism Education in Oakland, California, who first urged me to travel to Mississippi; and to Ira Hadnot and Jeff Rivers, whose many stories planted the seed and whose contacts allowed me to take my first small steps on my journey in the South.

The support of Joseph H. Wheatly, director of the Mississippi Delta Council for Farm Worker Opportunities, and his willingness to devote his staff's time to guide me during my many visits, made much of this work possible. Thanks to Joseph N. Richardson, assistant director of the council, who was always there to answer questions, take my many phone calls, and share his knowledge and staff with me; to E. L. Martin, guide and new friend, who opened his home and family and shared his hopes and dreams and great barbecue on my many trips; and to my other friends at the council who spent endless hours driving the Delta roads, visiting clients and neighbors, and opening the many doors in the Delta community: Reverend E. T. Thomas, Maggi James, Joseph Spencer, Josephine Braggs, and, in the Rosedale office, Clotee Washington and Delthia Thomas.

I appreciate the guidance and conversation of many other community organizers, including Dr. Ann Brooks of the Tutwiler clinic, Sister Angela Susala, Sister Julian Betts, Nellie Johnson, Sister Rosa Monica-Mildred, and others whom I met often for a brief moment but who generously introduced me to others or pointed me in the right direction.

Special thanks to Ms. Keith Dockery of the Dockery Farms, who shared her life, allowed me to enter her world, and helped me to see the cotton harvest; to Jerome Murry, who introduced me to the many juke joints of the Delta and became my friend; and to Bill Ferris for his continuing support of this project and for his work in the region with the Center for the Study of the Southern Culture at the University of Mississippi in Oxford.

I am grateful to Professor Leon Litwack at the University of California, Berkeley, for his thoughts and advice; Sid Graves at the Delta Blues Museum; and Jim O'Neal at Rooster Blues Records, who helped with his knowledge of blues music and juke joints. I always appreciated the open door of F. Jack Hurley and Nancy Hurley, who greeted me like family and spent many hours talking about photography and who helped me make an easy transition from my Delta trips as I moved back into my own world.

My thanks to Bob Moses for taking the time to write the introduction, to Janet Moses for her help and encouragement, and to Dave Dennis for his assistance.

Many people helped with conversations about the photographs and were always there to listen to me talk about my work. I especially want to thank Michelle Vignes, Kerry Tremain, and Kim Komenich; Jocelyne Benzakin of J.B. Pictures, for her enthusiasm and her efforts to market the photographs worldwide so the story could be told; Paul Turounet, my assistant, who helped with darkroom matters and spent many hours talking with me about photography.

The fact that this volume can be published at an affordable price is due to the generosity of Bob and Gail Israel, Carl Levinson and the Max and Anna Levinson Foundation, Jack Jaffe of the Focus Infinity Fund, Ernst Wildi and Skip Cohen of the Victor Hasselblad company, the Bernard Osher Foundation, the Hardin Foundation, and the Pioneer Fund of the Smithsonian

Institution. My neighbor Loren Coles and my colleague Richard Reinhardt gave advice and help with fundraising contacts, for which I am grateful.

Thanks are due Steve Dietz of the National Museum of American Art, who offered ideas, support, and criticism of the ongoing project, and his partner, Janet Malotky, who always made me feel welcome and at rest in their home; Pete Daniel of the National Museum of American History at the Smithsonian, for his perspective on the Delta; Pilar Perez, for her work on the traveling show; and Charles Collins, for his enthusiasm, support, and advice in making the show happen.

My editor, Amy Pastan, has always offered her support and encouragement. I have enjoyed her ideas and the give and take that is so important in this process. Her assistant, Cheryl Anderson, could always be counted on to respond to any questions, inquiry, or need to move this project forward, usually on a moment's notice. Thanks also to Jack Kirshbaum, my production editor, whose intelligent editing was greatly appreciated.

Readers wishing to learn more about the welfare of people in the Mississippi Delta communities can contact the Mississippi Delta Council for Farm Worker Opportunities in Clarksdale or the Mississippi Community Foundation in Jackson.

FOREWORD
ROBERT MOSES

In the end my own way of dealing with the unsettling pictures in Ken's book is to frame them with thoughts from the song Bernice Johnson Reagon and Sweet Honey in the Rock sing about Ella Baker:

Ella's Song

We who believe in Freedom cannot rest

We who believe in Freedom cannot rest until it comes

"I'm a woman who speaks in a voice and I must be heard,

at times I can be quite difficult, I bow to no man's word."

It was Ella Baker who told us about Amzie Moore and Aaron Henry in the Delta. She gave their names to Jane Stembridge and me in July 1960 as we prepared to seek students from Alabama, Mississippi, and Louisiana to come that fall to a Snick conference. On February 1 of that year, southern black college students had plunged themselves, the South, and the nation into the sit-in movement. Their pictures on the front pages of the *New York Times* drew me in. I told myself, "They look like I feel."

It was also Ella who gave to the sit-in students space to be heard within a more far-reaching movement. She sent out a call to come to Raleigh, North Carolina, to meet at Shaw University on Easter weekend, April 15–17, 1960. The students came and she helped them to found an organization in which they could be the leaders, and which, like her, "could be quite difficult": the Student Nonviolent Coordinating Committee (Snick). Ella's actions, in years to come, helped me to understand how the voice of organizers differs from that of leaders.

Jane, a white southerner, attended that conference; she came from Union Theological School in New York City and left for Atlanta, Georgia, to run Snick's first office. I arrived in Atlanta that summer, to "see the movement for myself, up close." Jane and I took the names Ella gave us, and Jane wrote ahead to alert people that a representative of Snick might drop by to visit. I left on a Greyhound bus, first to Birmingham, Alabama, and then on to Clarksdale in the Mississippi Delta. Clarksdale is the seat of Coahoma County, and the first person I met in the Delta was Aaron Henry, president of the NAACP for the state and leader of the Clarksdale chapter. I got off the bus, went to the drugstore he owned, and introduced myself.

"Until the killing of Black men, Black mother's sons,

is as important as the killing of white men, white mother's sons."

We who believe in Freedom cannot rest.

Deep into Ken's book there is a striking photograph called River Baptism, Moon Lake, Coahoma County, Mississippi, 1989. In it African Church people redo an ancient spiritual event: And it came to pass in those days that Jesus came from Nazareth of Galilee and was baptized of John in the Jordan River. The photograph pictures for me the central dilemma of our lives: To overcome our slave conditions, we black people have to first overcome ourselves.

Deep in my own mind I carry an image of an event on the boardwalk at Atlantic City in August 1964. Members of the Mississippi Freedom Democratic Party (MFDP) and supporters from around the country gather around Fannie Lou Hamer, who is leading us all in freedom songs. Close around her are a young Bernice Johnson Reagon, a young Eleanor Holmes Norton, and Ella. They had come because the lives of Andrew Goodman and Mickey Schwerner were no less and no more important than that of James Chaney; they had come to state their belief in Freedom.

Fannie Lou Hamer worked a plantation about twenty miles from Cleveland, Mississippi, but I couldn't know about such a person as I got off the bus and walked to the post office in search of Amzie.

Amzie was from the hill country, born and raised in Tallahatchie County, on the edge of the Delta. He came to Cleveland as a young adult, left to fight the Japanese in Burma in World War II, and came back again to lead, in the fifties, the Cleveland NAACP and do janitorial work in the Cleveland post office. Amzie became my movement father; he explained to me about the modern form of lynching, but he also taught me to look at plantation conditions and to map a strategy for "first-class citizenship."

Amzie knew about Fannie Lou Hamer, that she existed somewhere in the Delta; he just didn't know who she was, nor, in those times, that she could be a woman. And, as I said, I couldn't have known. In the fall of 1960, Amzie loaded a few young people into his huge old Packard, drove to Atlanta to the Snick conference, and explained, so to speak, about all of this to young sit-in leaders: "No use sitting-in at lunch counters in the Delta," he might have said. "Not enough food on the table."

"To me young people come first, they have the courage where we fail

and if I can but shed some light as they carry us through the gale."

We who believe in Freedom cannot rest.

Within the year, Amzie's home at 614 Chrisman St. in Cleveland would become the beachhead from which student leaders would penetrate the Delta. But as for the state itself, the students would find their own way: Freedom Rides. They would take the Freedom Rides into the deep South and enter Mississippi officially . . . as Freedom Riders. The rides were actually started by an older generation of activists: James Farmer and Jim Peck of the Congress of Racial Equality (CORE) led riders onto a Greyhound bus on May 4, 1961. Even so, a young John Lewis from the Nashville student movement was among them. They slowly made their way from the nation's capital into the deep South, testing public accommodations as they went. But when they reached Anniston, Alabama, their bus was burned, and they failed to carry the rides any further. Only the Nashville student movement, it turned out, had the fire to match that of the burning bus. I watched it all unfold from a distance, searching the newspapers back in New York City, finishing up the last year of my contract to teach math to middle schoolers at the Horace Mann School in Riverdale, preparing myself to return to the Delta and work for Snick on Amzie's program.

John Lewis and other Nashville students had been meticulously trained by James Lawson in the philosophy and tactics of nonviolent protest. Jim arrived in Nashville in 1957 having been nurtured, in part, by pacifists in and around the Fellowship of Reconciliation. His "nonviolent workshops" were part of the work of the Nashville Christian Leadership Council, an affiliate of Dr. King's organization. When the bus burned in Anniston, the Nashville students, through their spokesperson Diane Nash, were the only ones who said exactly, without a blink, that the rides must not be stopped. On May 24, they led the rides from Montgomery into Jackson, and in July, when Hollis Watkins, Curtis Hayes, and I walked the dusty roads of Beartown, in McComb, Mississippi, little children would point us out and whisper, "There goes some Freedom Riders."

"That which touches me most is that I had a chance to work with people
    passing on to others that which was passed on to me."
We who believe in Freedom cannot rest.

Many of the people in this book could not have been watching as the riders entered Mississippi with their national guardsmen and their press. Twelve-year-old Veronica Heags, chopping cotton in Coahoma County, and thirty-year-old Shirley Clark on Sherard Plantation, chopping cotton since she was thirteen—they weren't born yet. Neither was Jimmie, 13, walking to a plantation faucet for water near an abandoned cotton gin in Tallahatchie, nor Leola Thomas' three children, living in one room and without water or an indoor toilet. Nor was Jo Ann, 19, with her baby in Sugar Ditch, or swing man Larry Carodine, 27, fifteen years in the gin.

But many others were. Certainly Miss Ruth Ann, 70, of Jonestown and Cleo Cotton, also

70, and Sweeper, 73, of Tunica—certainly they were watching. They were right in there with Fannie Lou Hamer, who, forty-five years old in 1962, had eyes glued on the riders. Certainly Ms. Hall, 87, of Bolivar County, Ms. Jammie B. Wilson, 76, of Robinsonville, and Willi Dodd, 71, at his barbershop in Tutwiller—certainly they were watching too.

Fannie Lou was born in the Delta into a sharecropping family on October 16, 1917, child number twenty. In 1942 she married Perry "Pap" Hamer, and together they worked cotton plantations year after year after year in Sunflower County. And then it came to pass that in May 1961 Freedom Riders from Nashville and the sit-in movement were baptized in Sunflower County at Parchman State Penitentiary, a stone's throw from where the Hamers worked on the plantations and Amzie had begun to do his own "passing on to others."

> "The older I get the better I know that the secret of my going on
>
>   is when the reins are in the hand of the young who dare to run against the storm."
>
> We who believe in Freedom cannot rest.

In that part of the Delta it was only Amzie who would open up his house to Freedom Riders. In less than a year they were out of jail and working the Delta out of 614 Chrisman St. In the summer of 1962, they fanned out into different Delta towns. James Jones went to Clarksdale to work with Aaron Henry, Emma Bell went to Greenville, and Mattie Bivens worked in Cleveland. Diane Nash married James Bevel and they lived in Amzie's house. Sam Block went to Greenwood, where it took him four months just to find a place to live. Colia Lidell and Dorie Ladner went with Charles McLaurin and Charlie Cobb into Ruleville, Sunflower County, where Mrs. Hamer attended their mass meetings.

On August 31, 1962, Amzie pressed into service an old school bus from Bolivar County, and we loaded about eighteen of the people that Ken pictures in this book, as well as Mrs. Hamer, and drove down to Indianola, the county seat of Sunflower County. We drove them all: sharecroppers and day laborers, cotton choppers and cotton pickers; all the Cleo Cottons, the John Henry Wrights, the Miss Ruth Anns, the Sweepers, the Ms. Halls, the Ms. Jammie B. Wilsons, the Willi Dodds, the Ms. Ada Swanns, the Daniel Smerlings, the Rubys, the Ruth Holdmans to "radish" to vote. As the bus rode from Ruleville to Indianola, Mrs. Hamer sang her heart out to them all so they could face the registrar, the governor, the senator, the attorney general, the president, the American people, and themselves.

And so it came to pass that Mrs. Hamer was baptized into the Freedom Rides and her song filled the air, in Ruleville, at the mass meetings; in Hattiesburg, marching around the Court House; in Jackson, at the state convention for the MFDP; in Atlantic City, at the 1964 Democratic National Convention: "This Little light of mine, I'm going to let it shine." That was Mrs. Hamer and her song, but the tyranny captured in Ken's book, as I said, led me in the end to Ella and her song.

"Not needing to clutch for power, not needing the light just to shine on me,

I need to be one in the number as we stand against tyranny."

We who believe in Freedom cannot rest,

we who believe in Freedom cannot rest until it comes.

DELTA TIME

Ms. Mattie Conner in the field. Tunica County, Mississippi, 1990.

Roadside sign. Bolivar County, 1989.

Millen Farms. Drew, Mississippi, 1991.

Connell and Company, Baugh Plantation. Mississippi Delta, 1990.

Pleasant Green Baptist Church. Humphreys County, Mississippi, 1991.

Abandoned plantation shack. Mississippi Delta, 1989.

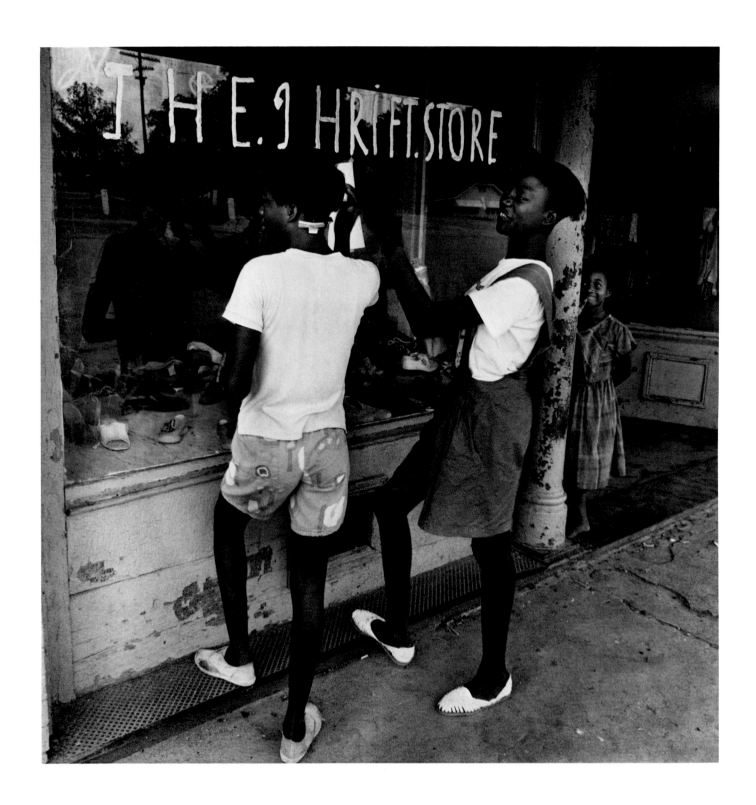

Saturday on Main Street. Duncan, Mississippi, 1992.

Cotton field along Highway 61. Mississippi Delta, 1990.

Jimmie, 13 years old, walking to a plantation faucet for water near an abandoned cotton gin.
Tallahatchie County, Mississippi, 1989.

Walking on Osley Avenue. Winstonville, Mississippi, 1991.

Anna May Rhodes with confederate flag scarf. Jonestown, Mississippi, 1989.

Cleo Cotton, 70 years old, in a home built by her father. Mississippi Delta, 1990.

Children of John Henry Wright, 63 years old. Off Highway 61. Mississippi Delta, 1989.

Leola Thomas, who has one room for her three children and no water or indoor toilet.
Glendora, Mississippi, 1989.

Bee Bop. Sugar Ditch Alley, Tunica, Mississippi, 1989.

Miss Ruth Ann, 70 years old. Jonestown, Mississippi, 1989.

Ms. Velma. De Soto Lake, Mississippi Delta, 1991.

"And it Came to Pass…" Sign along the road. Coahoma County, Mississippi, 1990.

Robert Johnson in his kitchen with no electricity or water. Walls, Mississippi, 1989.

Downtown on July 4. Sledge, Mississippi, 1992.

Downtown. Duncan, Mississippi, 1990.

On the porch, a hot summer day in August. Jonestown, Mississippi, 1989.

Cotton choppers, Sherard Plantation. Sherard, Mississippi, 1992.

Cotton chopper, earned $19.00 working 6 a.m.–12 noon. Coahoma County, Mississippi, 1991.

Shirley Clark, 30 years old, on Sherard Plantation, chopping cotton since she was 13. Sherard, Mississippi, 1992.

Harvesting cotton at the end of September. De Soto County, Mississippi, 1991.

"Old man Boyd" talks with one of his workers. Boyd Farms, Mississippi Delta, 1992.

Veronica Heags, 12 years old, chopping cotton, New Africa Road. Coahoma County, Mississippi, 1991.

Field worker, hot July day. Coahoma County, Mississippi, 1991.

Cotton. Mississippi Delta, 1991.

Claremont Gin Company, Adams Plantation. Coahoma County, Mississippi, 1992.

Field worker in cotton trailer, Dog Bog Road. Coahoma County, Mississippi, 1992.

Ginner's assistant at Claremont Gin Company, Adams Plantation. Coahoma County, Mississippi, 1990.

Larry Davis, 38 years old, earns $4.25/hour as a pressman on Sunday.
Dorothy Ann Gin Company, Tunica, Mississippi, 1991.

Cotton gin worker, Big Creek Gin. Lyon, Mississippi, 1990.

Field worker off Highway 61. Tunica, Mississippi, 1990.

Sweeper, 73 years old, Dorothy Ann Gin Company. Tunica, Mississippi, 1990.

Larry Carodine, swing man, 27 years old, fifteen years in the gin.
Farmers & Planters Gin, Tunica, Mississippi, 1992.

Dorothy Ann Gin. Tunica, Mississippi, 1990.

Gin worker, Midnight Cotton Gin. Midnight, Mississippi, 1992.

Cotton bales. Mississippi Delta, 1989.

Boys jumping on an old mattress. Gunnison, Mississippi, 1991.

Children without shoes ("The Dark Corner"). Dundee, Mississippi, 1989.

Willi Dodd, 71 years old, at his barber shop. Tutwiler, Mississippi, 1990.

Walking into town down the railroad tracks. Tutwiler, Mississippi, 1990.

On the porch of the plantation shack. Tunica County, Mississippi, 1989.

Jo Ann, 19 years old, and her baby. Sugar Ditch, Tunica County, Mississippi, 1989.

Young boy. Alligator, Mississippi, 1991.

Wearing his Sunday best. Coahoma County, Mississippi, 1989.

Ms. Hall, 87 years old. Bolivar County, Mississippi, 1989.

Ms. Jammie B. Wilson, 76 years old. Robinsonville, Mississippi, 1989.

Roderick, 4 years old, on his grandmother's lap. Rena Lara, Mississippi, 1992.

Young girl on her front steps. Bolivar County, Mississippi, 1992.

Walking home. Coahoma, Mississippi, 1992.

Ms. Ada Swann, 73 years old, in her kitchen. Rome, Mississippi, 1990.

Christina Anderson, 23 years old, with her children Caroline Antoinette, 5,
Christina, 3, and Cora, 5 months, in her $30 a month shack. Duncan, Mississippi, 1989.

Daniel Smerling, 71 years old, with his gun. Rich, Mississippi, 1989.

Van Coffey, 22 years old, with cotton patch rabbit shot with one shell. Duncan, Mississippi, 1989.

Mother and child, youngest of her six children. Duncan, Mississippi, 1990.

Jeanette Wallace, 9 months pregnant. Glendora, Mississippi, 1992.

Apostolic faith sign. Quitman County, Mississippi, 1990.

Mt. Nebo Missionary Baptist Church. Tunica County, Mississippi, 1989.

Sunday service, Faith Temple Word of Faith. Tutwiler, Mississippi, 1990.

Elder John Irving, Jr., Sunday preaching. Faith Temple Word of Faith. Tutwiler, Mississippi, 1990.

Holy roller, Faith Temple Word of Faith. Tutwiler, Mississippi, 1990.

Pleasant Grove Missionary Baptist Church. Coahoma, Mississippi, 1989.

Parishioner, Pleasant Grove Missionary Baptist Church. Coahoma County, Mississippi, 1989.

Parishioner with Bible. Coahoma County, 1989.

Grave digger, paid $30 to dig a grave 8 feet long x 4½ feet deep. Tunica, Mississippi, 1989.

Waiting to be baptized in Moon Lake. Coahoma County, Mississippi, 1989.

River baptism, Moon Lake. Coahoma County, Mississippi, 1989.

Baptism in Moon Lake. Coahoma County, Mississippi, 1989.

"Then cometh Jesus…" Marks, Mississippi, 1989.

Walking on the plantation road. Walls, Mississippi, 1989.

Kevin, 15 years old, looking out his screen door. Walls, Mississippi, 1992.

W. C. Stanton, 81 years old, who picked 300 pounds of cotton on a good day. Mississippi Delta, 1990.

Mother and four children. Glendora, Mississippi, 1991.

Leola Page with her three sons and grandbaby. Duncan, Mississippi, 1989.

Grocery store and Mr. Morrow's Oldsmobile. Hitt Spur, Mississippi, 1992.

Ruby, 61 years old, and James, 31 years old. Clayton, Mississippi, 1990.

Hoeing the garden. Walls, Mississippi, 1991.

Daisey Woodson with radio. Old Five Mile Road, Humphreys County, Mississippi, 1992.

Mr. Bucklesy. Shelby, Mississippi, 1990.

Cool Breeze Bar-B-Q. Quitman County, Mississippi, 1989.

Juke joint. Lula, Mississippi, 1992.

Dancing Saturday night at Margaret's Blue Diamond Club. Clarksdale, Mississippi, 1991.

Listening to the blues. Mississippi Delta.

Johnnie Billington playing the blues at Mt. Bayou Club. Mississippi Delta, 1992.

Saturday night at Margaret's Blue Diamond Club. Mississippi Delta, 1992.

Pool hall. Farrell, Mississippi, 1989.

Outside of the King Curtis Cafe. Lambert, Mississippi, 1990.

"Lawn jockey," off Highway 49. Mississippi Delta, 1991.

Main Street. Rosedale, Mississippi, 1992.

Dorothy, 8 years old, combing her doll's hair on her porch. Lyon, Mississippi, 1992.

KKK on television. Mississippi Delta, 1990.

Convict work gang, Parchman State Penitentiary, repairing the street. Drew, Mississippi, 1992.

Convict field workers, Parchman State Penitentiary, drinking water in 96 degree heat. Mississippi Delta, 1992.

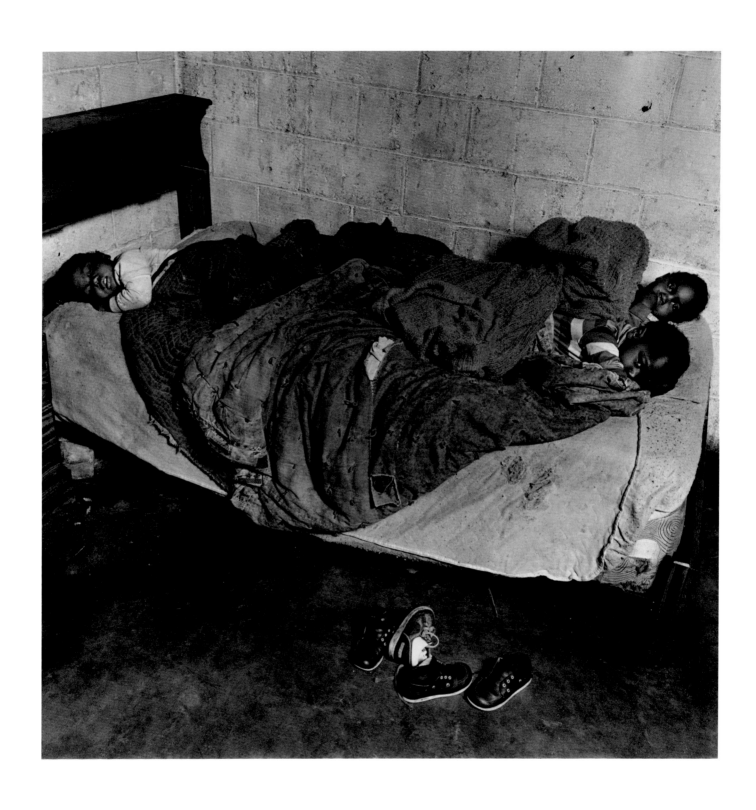

Children in their bed. Sugar Ditch Alley, Tunica, Mississippi, 1989.

Ruth Holdman, 70 years old, eating dinner. Jonestown, Mississippi, 1989.

Walking the dog. Marigold, Mississippi, 1990.

Mother and daughter, off Highway 61. Walls, Mississippi, 1990.

R.I.P. LeRoy Mackey. Tutwiler, Mississippi, 1991.

Hearse along Highway 49. Coahoma County, Mississippi, 1991.

AFTERWORD

KEN LIGHT

Everywhere the eye looks, the fields lining U.S. Highway 61 are exploding with large bulbs of cotton. The air is heavy with heat and humidity, and my mind's eye visualizes hundreds of black sharecroppers being swallowed into these fields, sweating from their brows, the years of hard labor chiseled in their faces, dragging heavy cotton bags laden with "King Cotton." In this poorest of places, in this land of opportunity called America, we see the best and worst of ourselves. The Mississippi Delta is a land where ghosts of the past still collide with the reality of twentieth-century America.

For me and my generation, Mississippi had become a symbol of the failures of American society. The images of generations of photographers are burned into our consciousness. I vividly recall the issues of *Life* magazine, with the National Guardsmen's bayonets fixed protecting the Freedom Riders from mobs of angry white townspeople and the buses being attacked. I remember the summer of 1964, being glued to my parents black-and-white television, waiting for word on the fate of civil rights workers Michael Schwerner, James Chaney, and Andrew Goodman. The drama of the FBI, Justice Department, and President Lyndon Johnson held this young viewer like some Hollywood movie. Could it be true that in America, in the state of Mississippi, three young men could be murdered fighting for rights that I had been taught were protected by the Constitution.

Rural Mississippi has often been described as a closed society, a world in which the Klan operated freely. Stories abound both in history and legend of the terror that was brought upon its people. The terror includes the brutal murder of Emmett Till, a black teenager who in 1955 went to visit his grandparents in LaFlore County and was lynched for allegedly whistling at a white woman. His body was thrown into the Tallahatchie River. This and other stories are burned into the consciousness of the Delta's small communities.

These childhood visions of television and my adult consciousness of the civil rights period filled me with anticipation as my car crossed from Memphis, Tennessee, into Mississippi in the dead of night.

In my four-and-a-half-year journey along Highway 61 and the smaller, less-traveled roads of the Delta, scenes that I thought had long vanished from this American land were revealed. Nothing had prepared me for this. The cypress-planked shotgun shack still sits on the edge of the plantation. Every day brings a new vision and new dismay in witnessing the lives of Delta people. These contrasting and dramatic forces create an overwhelming picture in the mind's eye, and an opportunity and responsibility. Few outsiders would believe what I have seen if not for my camera.

I had heard about Sugar Ditch, a community located in Tunica, Mississippi, which was slowly being dismantled because the sewage system was an open canal that ran behind the many homes that remained. I remember walking along the alley way behind the downtown, camera at my side, and coming upon a tall, skinny man with his hair greased down. I introduced myself and carefully looked at the cinder block homes he was standing next to, with dilapidated screen doors, often secured with a small hasp and old, almost nonfunctional locks. It looked as if these apartments were vacant.

But Bee Bop, the name he went by, informed me that this was his home as well as the home of many families. He offered to take me inside and introduce me to some of the others who lived there. I began to think about how I would make a photograph that fully described my own feeling of hopelessness. As I began to take a light reading and think about how to make a photograph, I realized that Bee Bop, despite his lack of possessions, had a great deal of presence and sense of himself that was outside of his living environment. He knew who he was. As I continued to travel, this side of the Delta revealed itself again and again.

One Friday as E. L. Martin and I drove back to Clarksdale after an afternoon of photographing, he turned to me and said that I had been invited to a river baptism at Moon Lake the following Sunday. I could hardly contain myself. His invitation had come after I had spent more than a year working in the Delta. As the time approached, I grew more and more excited at the prospect of witnessing this important religious confirmation. My mind raced with the visual images of what I might find. I had learned from previous trips that the Delta always seemed to hold a mysterious presence that revealed itself when it wanted to; nothing could be rushed. Clearly this invitation was a confirmation of this notion.

Sunday arrived, and my attention was focused on the people who were slowly gathering on the banks of Moon Lake. Many greeted me as old friends from previous photographic sessions; others knew I was a welcome guest. I watched as young girls were outfitted with handmade baptismal gowns sewn by their mothers. I could see on their faces the fear of the unknown, their excitement. I moved close with my camera, waiting for the instant that they seemed suspended in their own thoughts, as if they were physically outside of the actual ritual.

The girls slowly moved down the handmade steps from the bluff above the lake to the water's edge. The deacons moved with great seriousness and pride, guiding those about to be baptized into the water. As the deacons began to talk and pray, their voices rose, surrounding the young church members with their words, and I could see and feel the power they held. I began to understand the church and its meaning for these people, and how the rituals and celebrations allowed the human side of the Delta to survive the many violations of human dignity I had previously witnessed.

I watched as the light softened, the towering cypress trees casting a shadow on selected parts of the water, the white gowns forming a perfect line. I felt the spirit of the moment as I slowly released the shutter.

There often were mysterious moments. Many were laden with great power and some held great sadness. The people and events I encountered left me thinking that no amount of conscious or unconscious thought could have prepared me for what these roads held. As my visits extended over the years, I met people whose faces were powerful portraits that looked deeply into my camera lens.

Miss Ruth Ann is a small women with deep features chiseled into her face. The years have not been kind to her. In her dark one-room shack, heated by a cast-iron potbellied stove, she prepares the food her neighbors bring to her because she has no refrigerator. She rarely leaves the mounds of quilts that provide her warmth. Yet there is much evidence of a once vital life. Old photographs hang dirty and ripped, as in so many Delta homes, reminders of the days of sharecropping, before the mechanization of cotton forced hundreds of thousands of Delta field hands to migrate to the urban centers and changed their way of life and ours as well.

Delta residents like Miss Ruth Ann welcome me into their homes, some hoping that this visitor can explain why after a lifetime of picking cotton they are ineligible for Social Security payments. They point to a hole in the roof of their shotgun shack and ask that a picture be taken so that those outside the Delta world might see this legacy of rural poverty. In their homespun philosophy they often talk of how "the Lord has made a way for me." They are well aware of the years of neglect and disinterest on the part of local and federal governments, and yet they tolerate it, relying on their spiritual tradition to soothe the pain and rationalize their disenfranchisement.

W. C. Stanton, a large proud man who has lived most of his eighty-one years in Coahoma County, is quite humble that in his day he could pick three hundred pounds of cotton. Like many Delta residents, his feelings are direct and pointed. "Mississippi was a bad state for the colored folks. They were mistreated. If you wanted to live, you kept your mouth shut and your eyes closed." When questioned about how times have changed, he looks you squarely in the eyes, tightens his grasp on his long-handled hoe, and responds without skipping a beat, "White folks are still white folks; we are still treated like Negroes." As his words resound in my mind, I think about this man standing opposite me, witness to changes that have profoundly altered American life yet so little altered his world. There is still a black side of town and a cemetery for white's only. Schools are largely segregated, with many whites going to private academies, often named after confederate Civil War heroes.

The dignity and traditions of the Delta's people create a powerful presence that gives hope and pride to their hard lives. Their sadness and their humanity have struck me deeply and taught me that with my "freedom" to see and photograph comes a responsibility to listen.

Over the last twenty-four years, my education has been through the viewfinder of my camera. It has taken me to the heart of America. I have witnessed seven-year-old children in America's agricultural fields picking tomatoes for 34 cents a bucket. I have watched in total darkness as thousands of undocumented aliens have run and been chased across U.S. borders. I have photographed third world countries and urban poverty in America. I can truly say that nothing has torn at me so heavily as what I saw in Mississippi. The people of the Delta have allowed me to look deeper into my own world and into myself. I have realized that Mississippi can be a window for us all, our hopes and our fears. As we enter the twenty-first century, I have often wondered why their plight has been ignored, why their desire for freedom from want and their voices go unheard and unanswered.

I think back to those days as I watched my parents TV, thirteen years old and drawn by the fears for the missing civil rights workers and of what I saw. I think of the hopes that I held in my heart. Surely, America wouldn't turn its eyes from places such as the Mississippi Delta.

TECHNICAL INFORMATION

All of the photographs in this volume were taken with a Hasselblad 500CM using numerous backs and a 60mm, 50mm, 150mm, or occasionally a 250mm lens. The camera and negative format allowed for the critical sharpness of the photographs. Exposure readings were made with a Pentax spot meter.

Many of the interior images were illuminated with a Norman 200B mounted on a light stand using an umbrella and calculating exposure with a Minolta III flash meter or a hand-held Vivitar 285 flash powered with a Quantum battery.

All the photographs were made with Kodak's Tri-X Pan and Panatomic-X or Verichrome Pan. The film was developed in D-76 with Crone Additive, which holds and expands the shadow details. The film and prints were developed by the photographer between 1989 and 1993 in his darkroom. All the prints were made on Agfa Insignia paper, archivally printed with Neutol developer and selenium-toned.

This book was acquired by Amy Pastan for Smithsonian Institution Press. The book was edited by Jack Kirshbaum and designed by Linda McKnight. Production was managed by Ken Sabol. Type was composed with QuarkXPress software for Macintosh by Linda McKnight using the Univers family of typefaces from Adobe Systems. Duotone film was made by Thomas Palmer of Newport, Rhode Island. The book was printed and bound by The Stinehour Press of Lunenburg, Vermont.